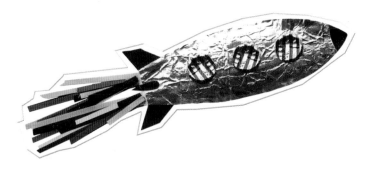

BLAST OFF!
SATURN

Helen and David Orme

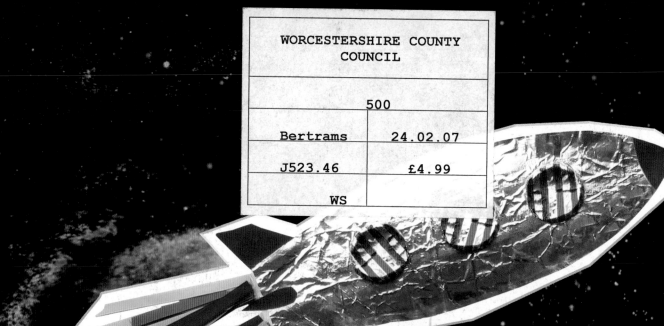

Copyright © ticktock Entertainment Ltd 2007
First published in Great Britain in 2006 by ticktock Media Ltd.,
Unit 2, Orchard Business Centre, North Farm Road,
Tunbridge Wells, Kent, TN2 3XF

ticktock project editor: Julia Adams
ticktock project designer: Emma Randall

We would like to thank: Sandra Voss, Tim Bones, James Powell,
Indexing Specialists (UK) Ltd.

ISBN 978 1 84696 053 6
Printed in China
A CIP catalogue record for this book is available from the British Library.

Picture credits
t=top, b=bottom, c=centre, l-left, r=right, bg=background
Mary Evans Picture Library: 16bl; NASA: 1tl, 1br, 6/7bg, 7tr, 7bl, 9tl, 10/11bg, 11bl, 13br, 14/15bg, 14tr, 14cr, 15tr, 18/19bg,
19tl, 19tr, 20bl, 21tl, 21br, 22/23bg, 22c, 23tl, 23br; NASA/Erich Karkoschka: 15bl; NASA/JPL/SSI: 1tl, 15bl; Science Photo
Library: front cover, 4/5bg (original), 8bl, 13tl, 17br; Shutterstock: 2/3bg, 7cr, 14cr, 24bg; ticktock picture archive: 5tr, 6bl, 9bl,
10bl, 12c, 17tl, 17bl, 18tr, 18cl, 18cr, 18br
Every effort has been made to trace the copyright holders, and we apologise in advance for any unintentional omissions.
We would be pleased to insert the appropriate acknowledgements in any subsequent edition of this publication.

Contents

Where is Saturn? 4-5

Planet Facts 6-7

The Weather on Saturn 8-9

Saturn's Amazing Rings 10-11

Saturn's Amazing Moons 12-13

Saturn's Biggest Moon 14-15

Saturn in History 16-17

What Can We See? 18-19

Missions to Saturn 20-21

Future Missions 22-23

Glossary and Index 24

Where is Saturn?

There are eight planets in our **solar system**. The planets travel around the Sun. Saturn is the sixth planet from the Sun.

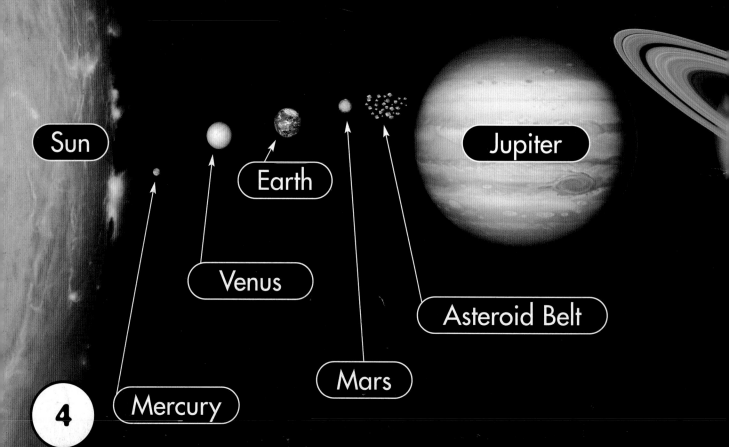

Sun

Mercury

Venus

Earth

Mars

Asteroid Belt

Jupiter

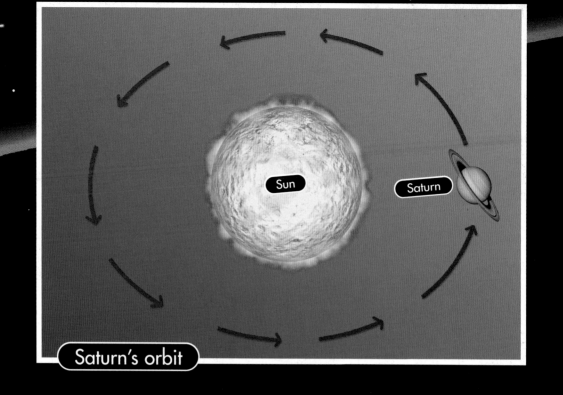

Sun

Saturn

Saturn's orbit

Saturn travels around the Sun once every 29½ **Earth years**. This journey is called its **orbit**. The time it takes for a planet to travel around the Sun once is called a **year**.

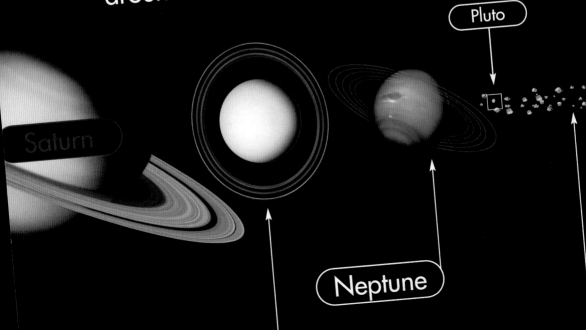

Pluto

Saturn

Neptune

Planet Facts

Saturn is the second-biggest planet in the **solar system**. For its size, it is also the lightest in weight. Saturn is one of the 'gas giant' planets.

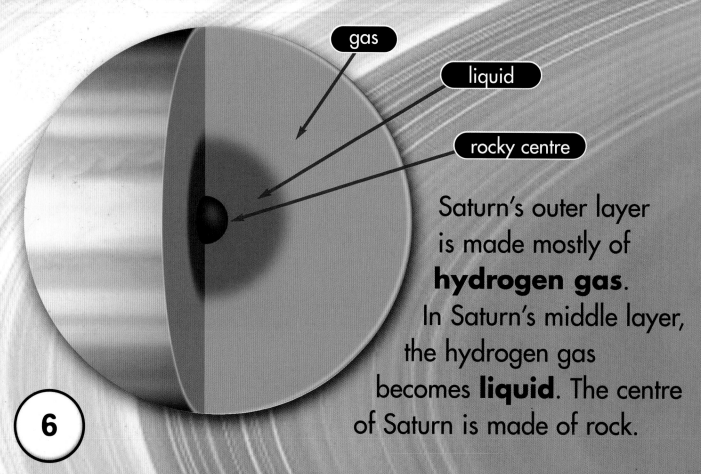

gas

liquid

rocky centre

Saturn's outer layer is made mostly of **hydrogen gas**. In Saturn's middle layer, the hydrogen gas becomes **liquid**. The centre of Saturn is made of rock.

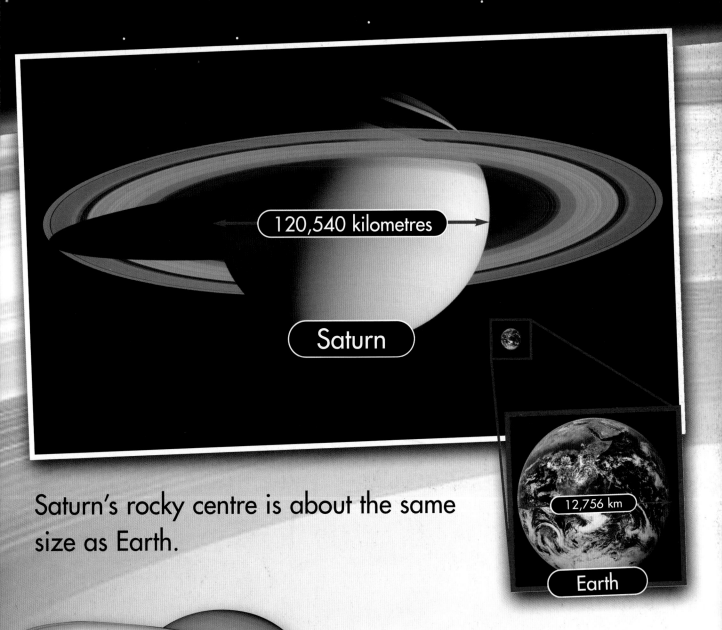

120,540 kilometres

Saturn

Earth

12,756 km

Saturn's rocky centre is about the same size as Earth.

Planets are always spinning. The time it takes a planet to spin around once is called a **day**. A day on Saturn is 10½ hours long on Earth!

Saturn is a very stormy place. The winds can travel at 1170 km per hour! The fastest winds recorded on Earth reached 512 km per hour.

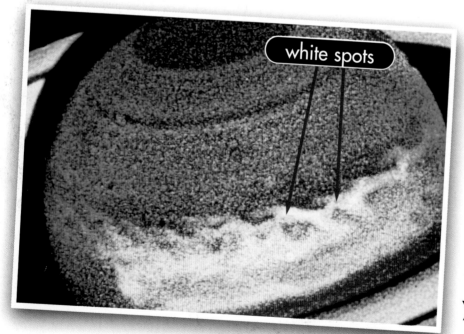

white spots

The storms on Saturn look like great white spots. Scientists have been watching the great white spots for 100 years.

Scientists say the storms happen every 30 years, but they don't know why.

Dragon Storm

Another large storm on Saturn is called Dragon Storm, because of its shape. The Dragon Storm is a giant thunderstorm. It produces lightning, just like a storm on Earth.

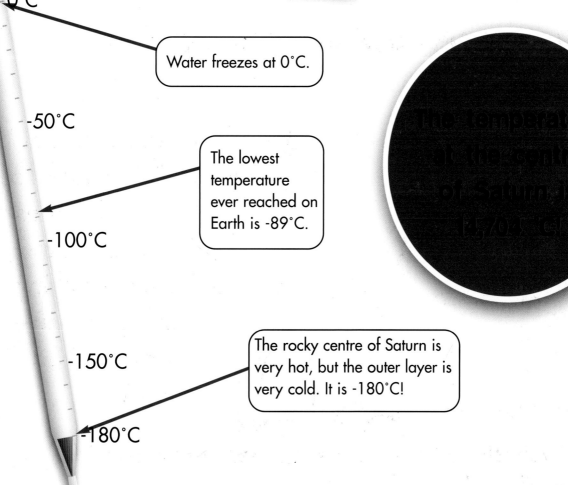

0°C

Water freezes at 0°C.

-50°C

The lowest temperature ever reached on Earth is -89°C.

-100°C

The temperature at the centre of Saturn is 11,704°C!

The rocky centre of Saturn is very hot, but the outer layer is very cold. It is -180°C!

-150°C

-180°C

Saturn's Amazing Rings

Saturn has the largest and brightest system of rings in the **solar system**. The rings are made of ice with some dust and rock.

Some chunks of dirty ice are as big as a house!

There are seven rings around Saturn. Some are very small and difficult to see.

Some rings are very thin. They are only about 9 metres thick. That's about the height of a 2 storey house!

The big rings are made up of many smaller ringlets.

The large dark stripes are the gaps between the rings.

rocks that **orbit** a planet. Only one moon orbits Earth, but at least 56 moons orbit Saturn! **Astronomers** are still finding new ones today.

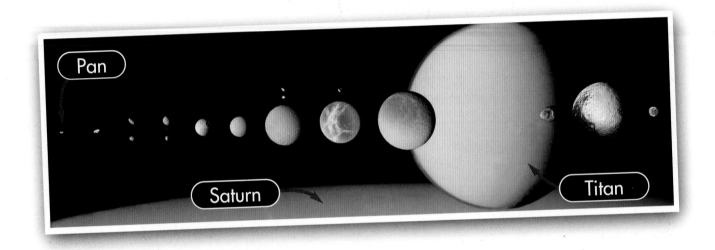

Pan

Saturn

Titan

Saturn has moons of many sizes. Pan is the smallest moon that has been discovered. It is 256 times smaller than Titan. Titan is Saturn's largest moon.

Small moons near the edges of Saturn's rings are called shepherd moons.

Iapetus is a very strange moon because one half of the surface is coloured white. The other half of the surface is a dark reddish colour. The white half has lots of ice on the surface. Scientists don't know why the other half is dark, though.

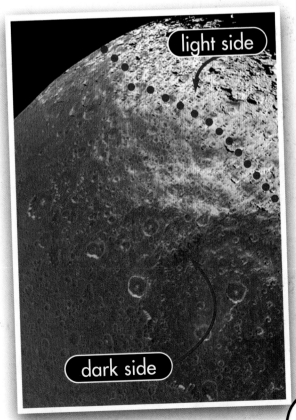

light side

dark side

Saturn's Biggest Moon

Saturn's biggest Moon is Titan. It is the second biggest moon in the **solar system**! It is about half the size of Earth.

5150 km

Titan

12,756 kilometres

Earth

atmosphere

Titan

Titan is very unusual because it has a thick **atmosphere**. Scientists think Earth's atmosphere was like this millions of years ago.

Astronomers discovered flat areas, or lakes, on Titan. But the lakes are not made of water. Titan is very cold. Its lakes are made of gases so cold they become liquid.

This artist's drawing shows what Titan's surface might look like.

These are two photographs of Titan's surface. They were taken by the **orbiter** Cassini in 2006. The dark spots are the lakes on Titan.

No other planet or moon in the solar system except Earth has lakes on its surface!

Saturn in History

Saturn was well known in ancient times. It is the furthest planet that can be seen from Earth without a telescope.

This painting shows the Roman god Saturn. People in ancient Rome believed that he was the god of farming. They named the planet Saturn after him.

Galileo Galilei was an Italian **astronomer**. He built his own telescopes to study the sky. When Galileo looked at Saturn through his telescope in 1610, he saw two lumps on either sides of Saturn. He called them the 'ears of Saturn'.

In 1656, the Dutch astronomer Christiaan Huygens viewed Saturn through a more powerful telescope. He discovered the 'ears of Saturn' were actually rings!

What Can We See?

From Earth, Saturn looks like a bright yellow star. It is easy to see without a telescope.

Saturn

Moon

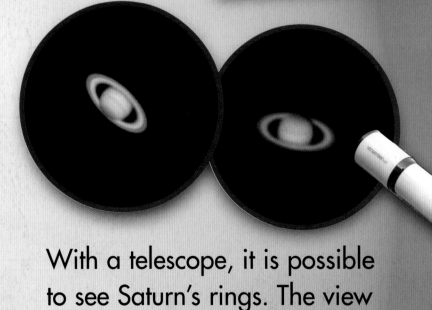

With a telescope, it is possible to see Saturn's rings. The view of the rings depends on which way Saturn is tilting.

Some telescopes **orbit** the Earth and take pictures from space. Telescopes in space take very clear pictures. The Hubble Space Telescope takes many pictures of space objects, such as planets and stars.

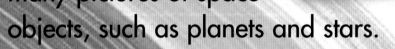

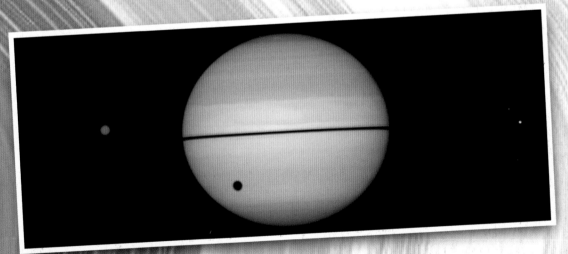

Saturn does not always look the same. The Hubble Space Telescope took a picture of Saturn that makes the rings look like a flat line! The dots are Saturn's larger moons.

Missions to Saturn

The most important mission to Saturn is Cassini-Huygens. The mission is made up of the **orbiter** Cassini and the **space probe** Huygens.

the rocket lanching Cassini-Huygens

At the beginning, of the mission, Huygens was attached to Cassini. They were taken to space by a rocket. The rocket was launched in 1997. It reached Saturn in July 2004.

Saturn

Huygens   Cassini

In December 2004, the Cassini-Huygens spacecraft seperated into two space probes.

Cassini began orbiting Saturn to study the planet from space.

Saturn

Huygens

Cassini

Titan

The Huygens space probe was sent to Titan. It travelled down through Titan's **atmosphere** to find out about the moon.

In this painting, we can imagine what someone standing on Titan might see.

Future Missions

Titan has an **atmosphere**, just like Earth's was millions of years ago. **Astronomers** would like to find out more about Titan, because this will help us understand more about how the Earth developed.

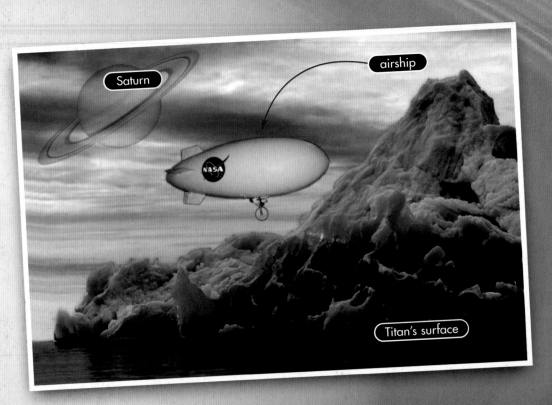

Saturn

airship

NASA

Titan's surface

A future spacecraft might float in Titan's thick atmosphere. It could look like the craft pictured here.

Enceladus

Scientists would like Cassini to do an extra mission and study the moon Enceladus in more detail.

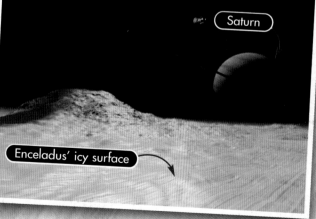

Saturn

Enceladus' icy surface

The surface of Enceladus is covered in ice. There might be **liquid** water under the ice. Where there is liquid water, there might be life!

Glossary

Asteroid A rocky object that orbits the Sun. Most asteroids orbit the Sun between Mars and Jupiter.

Astronomers People who study space, often using telescopes.

Atmosphere The gases that surround a star, planet or moon.

Day A day is the time it takes a planet to spin around once. A day on Earth is 24 hours long.

Earth year A year is the time it takes for a planet to orbit the Sun. An Earth year is 365 days long.

Hydrogen gas A very light gas. The Sun is also made of Hydrogen.

Liquid Something that flows easily.

Orbit The path that a planet or other object takes around the Sun, or a satellite takes around a planet.

Orbiter A spacecraft designed to go into an orbit around a planet. It takes pictures of the planet and sends them back to Earth.

Solar system The Sun and everything that is in orbit around it.

Space probe A spacecraft sent from Earth to explore the solar system. It can collect samples and take pictures.

Year The time it takes a planet to orbit the Sun.

Index

astronomers 15, 17, 22

atmosphere 14, 22

Cassini orbiter 15, 20–21, 23

Earth 7, 14

Enceladus 23

history 16–17

Huygens space probe 20–21

hydrogen 6

Iapetus 13

ice 10, 23

lakes 15

missions 20–23

moons 12–15, 19, 21, 23

orbiters 15, 20–21, 23

orbits 5, 12

Pan 12

planets 4–7

rings 10–11, 18–19

solar system 4–6

space probes 20–21

storms 8–9

telescopes 17–19

temperature 9

Titan 12, 14–15, 21–22

water 23

weather 8–9